WHICH "B" DO YOU SEE?

CREATED BY: Xel

ARTWORK BY: Xel

LITERATURE BY: Xel

EDITED BY: Xel

RESEARCH BY: Xel

"BEE FRIENDS SONG"

No matter what I use to be, everyday's a chance for me, to be the "B" I want to be because I've learned what's best for me, I'll be your friend, you'll be my friend, let's all be friends"BEE FRIENDS"!

When we all get a treat,

and I get mine to keep,

but I want one for now

to eat, so I say to you

"YOU'D BETTER NOT TATTLE,"

then I take your treat.

    DO YOU KNOW,

    CAN YOU SEE,

     WHICH "B"

    NAMES ME?

When we all get a treat, I'll keep mine because I'm a keeper, then I see you letting someone take yours cause you feel weaker. It's not happening to me is why I won't tell our teacher.

    DO YOU KNOW,
    CAN YOU SEE,
      WHICH "B"
    NAMES ME?

When we all get a treat, and I'm enjoying the one that's meant for me, I see someone take yours, so I report what shouldn't be.

DO YOU KNOW,

CAN YOU SEE,

WHICH "B"

NAMES ME?

FACT: A snitch is someone who does wrong then tattle on others for doing the same things, if you're not doing bad things but others do them to you; you're a victim who must report them.

I've been taught that school is a place I go to respect everyone, learn more and do what's right. I choose to be disrespectful, pick on others and fight.

    DO YOU KNOW,
    CAN YOU SEE,
     WHICH "B"
    NAMES ME?

I've been taught that school is a place I go to be happy learning, never judge others and feel safe. I stay distracted and afraid because I'm picked on most days. I don't ask for help; I'm sad to say, cause I keep hoping the problems go away.

    DO YOU KNOW,

    CAN YOU SEE,

      WHICH "B"

    NAMES ME?

I've been taught that school is a place I go that will make my brain get smarter and make my knowledge grow. I will always report anyone doing wrong to me when I'm here because that's a NO-NO.

DO YOU KNOW,
CAN YOU SEE,
WHICH "B"
NAMES ME?

FACT: Young bullies who don't get reported began to think their victims would become comfortable to being bullied.

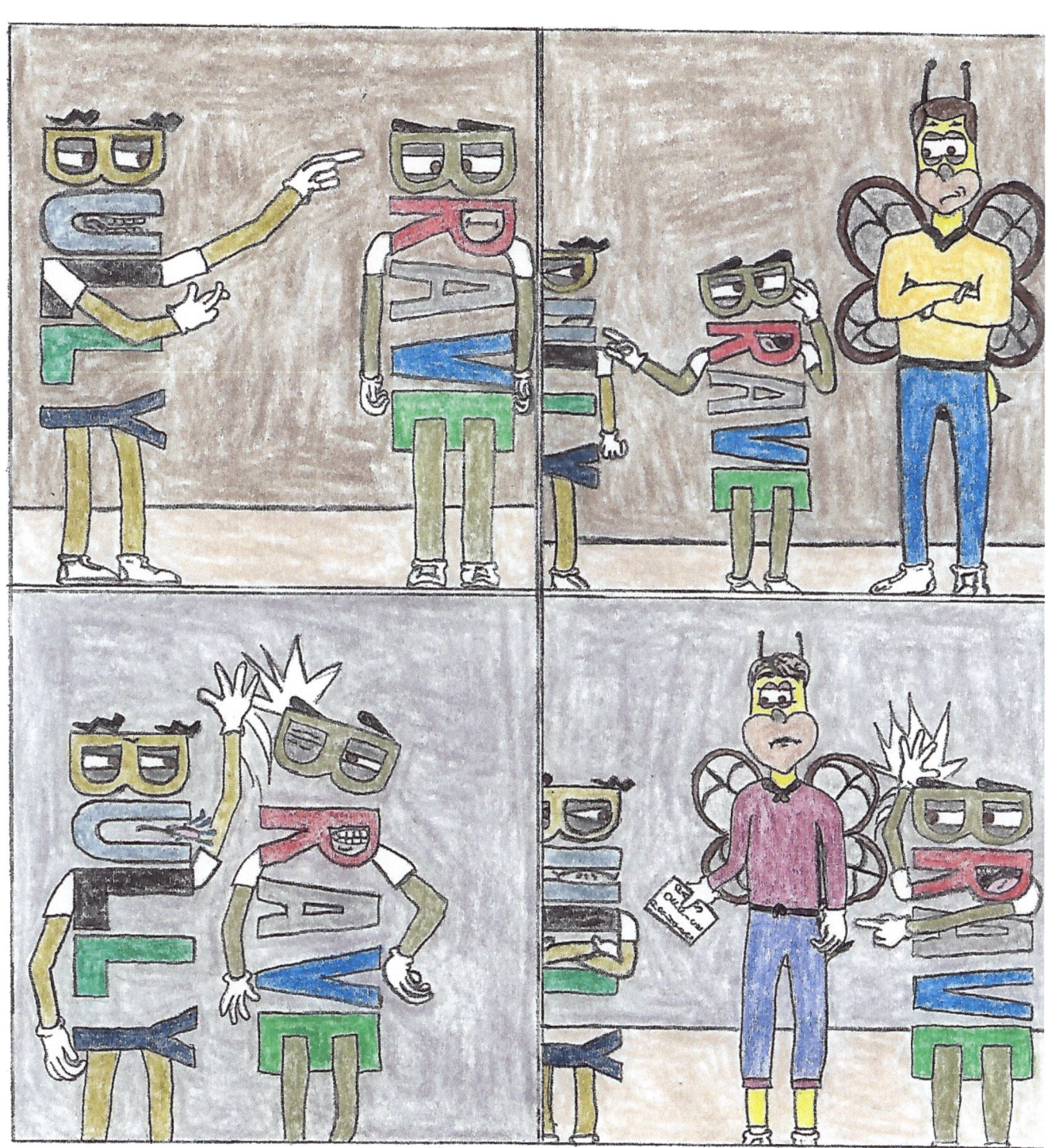

I eat breakfast at home and bring my lunch to school, I then make fun of those eating from the cafeteria when I know it's cruel.

DO YOU KNOW,
CAN YOU SEE,
WHICH "B"
NAMES ME?

It's hard for me to do my class work when I'm hungry, I could have eaten from the cafeteria, but I didn't because some would have made fun of me.

    DO YOU KNOW,
    CAN YOU SEE,
      WHICH "B"
    NAMES ME?

Food is smart fuel and if I don't have time to eat from home I will eat at school. I don't care what anyone may say because treating myself right is the correct thing to do and that's what's cool.

DO YOU KNOW,

CAN YOU SEE,

WHICH "B"

NAMES ME?

FACT: Never let anyone make you feel bad or wrong for doing what's right, bullies will try but bullying is what's bad and wrong.

As a teacher, my job is to teach and treat all my students the same, but I have my favorites that I treat like a prince and princess and the others I treat plain.

DO YOU KNOW,
CAN YOU SEE,
WHICH "B"
NAMES ME?

As a teacher, my job is to teach and treat all my students the same, so no matter your name, looking over your work confused is not asking me for help, that's why I let you figure it out yourself.

DO YOU KNOW,
CAN YOU SEE,
WHICH "B"
NAMES ME?

As a teacher, my job is to teach and treat all my students the same, so no teacher's pets will I claim, and if you don't understand your work nor ask for help, I'll still help because I'll detect it myself.

DO YOU KNOW,
CAN YOU SEE,
WHICH "B"
NAMES ME?

FACT: Teachers who make differences with students can make bullies of them without knowing.

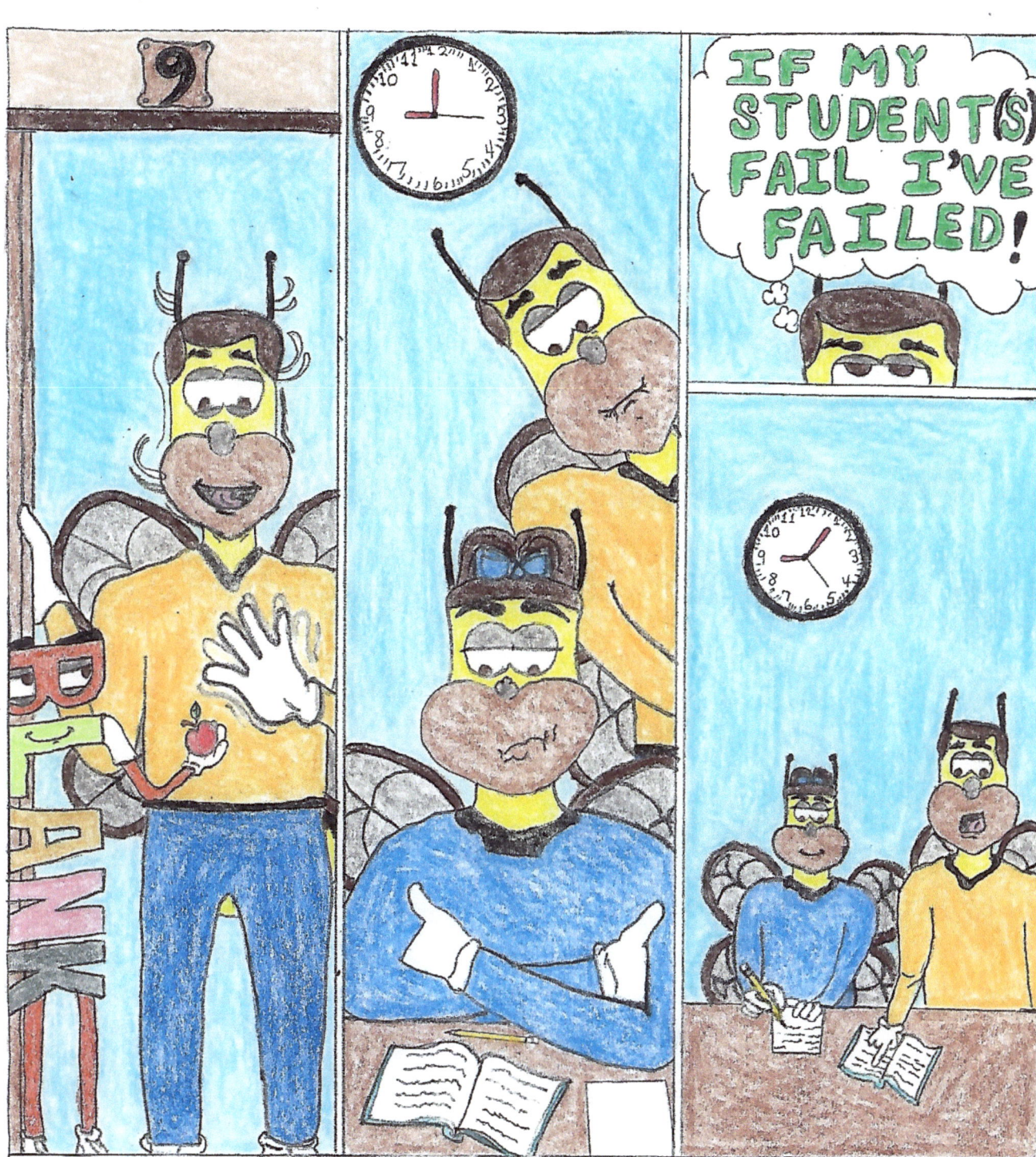

As a teacher, my job is never let my personal life reach my students, but if I'm disliked by, or I don't like some of their family members, I'll never admit it, but I won't treat or be fair to those students, and I'll blame them for most bad incidents.

    DO YOU KNOW,
    CAN YOU SEE,
      WHICH "B"
      NAMES ME?

As a teacher, my job is never let my personal life reach my students, so when I'm having a bad day I'll substitute their education with some fun amusements.

DO YOU KNOW,
CAN YOU SEE,
 WHICH "B"
NAMES ME?

As a teacher, my job is never let my personal life reach my students, so if I'm disliked by, or I don't like some of their family members, positive and professionally am how I handle it; and no bad days will hinder what I must do for my students because I'm here for their improvements.

DO YOU KNOW,

CAN YOU SEE,

WHICH "B"

NAMES ME?

FACT: Students who learn things about their teachers personal life causes confusion and Alters their mind and concentration in their school work.

As a teacher, my job is to know some students don't learn as fast as others or learn the same, but I reward the fast learners making the slower learners feel like losers and ashame.

DO YOU KNOW,
CAN YOU SEE,
WHICH "B"
NAMES ME?

As a teacher, my job is to know some students don't learn as fast as others or learn the same, but I keep it simple and plain, I'll give you work and only once will I explain; so pay attention because the grades you make you"ll receive in my grade book next to your name.

    DO YOU KNOW,

    CAN YOU SEE,

      WHICH "B"

    NAMES ME?

As a teacher, my job is to know some students don't learn as fast as others or learn the same, so I always teach each student at a pace for gain because it's also my job to make sure they promote and not be retained.

DO YOU KNOW,
CAN YOU SEE,
WHICH "B"
NAMES ME?

FACT: Some students pay full attention to the teachers' example the first time and still don't understand. It will be very helpful if the teacher or a student who's correctly completed their assignment would give examples every 5 minutes.

You are a BRAND NEW YOU everyday you awake and that makes YOU SPECIAL.

Sincerely Thanks
Sincerely Thanks

www.ingramcontent.com/pod-product-compliance
Lightning Source LLC
Chambersburg PA
CBHW042027150426
43198CB00002B/90